Praying
Circles
Around Your
Children

Praying
Circles
Around Your
Children

Mark Batterson

ZONDERVAN.com/
AUTHORTRACKER
follow your favorite authors

ZONDERVAN

Praying Circles around Your Children
Copyright © 2012 by Mark Batterson

Requests for information should be addressed to:
Zondervan, *Grand Rapids, Michigan 49530*

Library of Congress Cataloging-in-Publication Data

Batterson, Mark.
      Praying circles around your children / Mark Batterson.
         p. cm.
      Includes bibliographical references
      ISBN 978-0-310-32550-5 (softcover)
      1. Parents — Religious life. 2. Parent and child — Religious
aspects — Christianity. 3. Intercessory prayer — Christianity.
4. Prayer — Christianity. I. Title.
BV4529.B3773   2012
248.3'2 — dc23   2012014711

Published in association with the literary agency of Fedd & Company, Inc., Post Office Box 341973, Austin, TX 78734.

Cover design: Extra Credit Projects
Interior illustration: iStockPhoto®
Interior design: Beth Shagene

Printed in the United States of America

---

12 13 14 15 16 17 /DPM/ 13 12 11 10 9 8 7 6 5 4 3 2 1

Contents

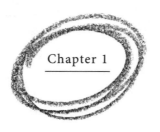

Chapter 1

The
Greatest *Legacy*
You Can Leave

I *want to be famous in my home.*

This is the deepest desire of my heart and the greatest challenge of my life. Parenting our three children is far more difficult and far more important than pastoring thousands of people. Just the other day, I said to Lora, "I feel like we'll finally figure out this parenting thing the same day our kids leave home!"

The truth is, we'll never figure it out, because children are moving targets. Just when you think you have them pegged, they become toddlers or teenagers or twentysomethings, and you're right back at square one. All you can do is learn a few lessons along the way and enjoy the journey. I have discovered one thing, however, that makes all the difference in the world.

Make sure the heavenly Father hears about your kids daily!

Bad News, Good News, and Great News

Right at the outset, let me give you some bad news, some good news, and some great news about parenting and praying for your children.

The bad news first: *You'll make a lot of mistakes.*

You'll lose your patience. You'll lose your temper. You might even lose your mind a time or two. If you feel like a failure at the end of most days, welcome to my world. My parenting ineptitude is epitomized by one shining moment when our oldest son, Parker, was a toddler. He had a fitful night full of tears, and I couldn't understand why.

Then he crawled into our room in the middle of the night. I was too tired to take him back to his bed, so I reached down to pull him into ours. That's when I realized why he had been crying. A bare butt was the tip-off that I had forgotten to put a diaper on him when I put him to bed.

It's amazing our kids even survive our parenting, isn't it?

While we're on the subject, the word *diaper* spelled backward is *repaid*. So apropos!

Now here's the good news: *Your worst mistakes double as your greatest opportunities.*

How will your kids learn to apologize unless you model it for them, to them? Your mistakes give you the opportunity to teach them one of the most important lessons they'll ever learn — how to say "I'm sorry."

I have a very simple parenting philosophy that boils down to just three words: *please*, *sorry*, and *thanks*. If all else fails, I want to teach my kids to be really good at saying these words. And then doing them. If they master these three words, they're well on their way to great marriages, great friendships, or great relationships with God.

Finally, here's the great news: *Prayer covers a multitude of sins.*

You don't have to do everything right as a parent, but there is one thing you cannot afford to get wrong. That one thing is prayer. You'll never be a perfect parent, but you can be a praying parent. Prayer is your highest privilege as a parent. There is nothing you can do that will have a higher return on investment. In fact, the dividends are eternal.

Prayer turns ordinary parents into prophets who shape the destinies of their children, grandchildren, and every generation that follows.

Prayer Genealogy

The blood running through my veins is 50 percent Swedish. I trace my genealogy back through the Johansson family, who made a decision to get on a boat and come to America in the late nineteenth century. That single decision set off a chain reaction that radically altered the destiny of every descendant to follow. That one decision made its mark on children, grandchildren, and great-grandchildren in more ways than I can possibly imagine.

Just as one decision can change your destiny, so can one prayer. If you were to map out your spiritual history, you would find countless answers to prayer at key intersections along the way. Before you were even born, even named, many of you had parents and grandparents who prayed for you. At critical ages and stages, family and friends interceded on your behalf. And thousands of complete strangers have prayed for you in ways you aren't even aware of. The sum total of those prayers is your prayer genealogy.

It's like your tree of life, your tree of Adam.

I believe that every blessing, every breakthrough, every miracle traces back to the prayers that were prayed by you or for you. One of the greatest moments in eternity will be the day God peels back the space-time curtain and unveils His sovereignty by connecting the divine dots between our prayers and His answers. That infinite web of prayer crisscrosses every nation, every generation. And when God finally reveals His strange and mysterious ways, it will drop us to our knees in worship. We will thank Him for the prayers He did answer. We'll also thank Him for the prayers He didn't answer because we'll finally understand why. And we'll thank Him for the answered prayers we weren't even aware of.

My grandfather Elmer Johnson died when I was just six years old, but his prayers did not. Our prayers never die. They live on in the lives of those we prayed for. Some of the most poignant and providential moments in my life have been the moments when the Spirit of God has whispered to my spirit, *Mark, the prayers of your grandfather are being answered in your life right now.*

My Grandpa Johnson had a habit of kneeling by his bed at night, taking off his hearing aid, and praying for his family. He couldn't hear himself, but everyone else in the house could. Few things are more powerful than hearing someone intercede on your behalf. His voiceprint left an imprint on my soul.

I'm following in my grandfather's foot-steps by getting on my knees and pray-ing next to my bed. It's a great way to start the day. My first thoughts and words are directed toward God. I also pray for my sleeping beauty lying a few feet away.

I realize not everyone inherited a prayer legacy from their parents or grandpar-ents like I did, but you can leave a legacy for future generations. You can start a new tradition, a new tree. You can begin a new prayer genealogy.

The Most Important Ten Minutes of the Day

The most important ten minutes of my day are the ten minutes I spend with my kids right before they leave for school. For many years, I felt like a failure when it came to leading my family in devotions. I could never seem to find a rhythm or a routine. It felt like one failed attempt after another. Then, the week before Parker started high school, Lora and I were on our Monday morning coffee date. Since I preach on Sundays, Monday is our Sabbath. We talk about our marriage, our kids, our calendar, and our finances. During the course of this particular conversation, I confessed my feeling of failure — and that's when Lora shared something her dad did, which I decided to adopt.

My father-in-law prayed with more intensity and more consistency than anybody I've ever known. That's why I dedicated *The Circle Maker* to Bob Schmidgall. He prayed about everything. In fact, when I asked him if I could marry his daughter, he literally said, "Let me pray about it." That'll put the fear of God in you! Especially when he didn't check back in for a week!

Bob Schmidgall was extraordinarily busy pastoring the church he founded in Naperville, Illinois, but he found time to do devotions with his four children every day before school. In the spirit of full disclosure, the teenaged Lora didn't always enjoy those devotions. What teenager does? But more than a decade after her dad's death, those times they spent together are treasured memories. Those devotions were a daily touchpoint with her dad.

One of the great challenges with family devotions is finding a consistent time and place to pray together. It's not easy when your kids are playing soccer, taking piano lessons, participating in a school club, and taking swim lessons. And that's probably just one of your children! So how do you find a rhythm? I think it starts with looking at your daily routines. It makes sense to pray with your young children before bed because you tuck them in every night. With older children, it's more difficult because they probably will be staying up later than you do.

When Lora shared the story about morning devotions with her dad, it was a revelation. I knew I needed to leverage the first few minutes of the day before the day got away from me. So beginning on Parker's first day of high school, I started reading the Bible and praying with him. Does every devotional time seem like a success? Hardly.

Are there days when we're running late and have to scoot out of the house? Absolutely. But I'm determined to have a daily devotion with my children, and this touch point is the most important ten minutes of my day. It's the most important meeting of the day. Why? Because I love my children so much more than anybody I'll meet with the rest of the day. And while every devotional time doesn't result in an epiphany, some of those touch points have turned into turning points.

Long After You Die

I know it's hard to find a consistent time and place to pray, but where there's a will, there's a way. And when it's God's will, God will help make a way.

Susanna Wesley gave birth to nineteen children, including John and Charles, the founders of the Methodist movement. There is no finding a quiet place to pray when you live in a small house with that many kids, but this reality didn't keep Susanna from praying. She would sit in her rocking chair in the middle of the living room, put a blanket over herself, and intercede for her children.

Our excuses just went away, didn't they? Your children need to see and hear you praying. It doesn't matter whether it's in a prayer closet or a prayer chair. You can turn your commute or your workout into prayer times. When you make their beds or fold their clothes, pray for them. Go into their bedrooms while they're sleeping, kneel next to their beds, and pray over them.

You don't become a praying parent by default. You do it by design, by desire, by discipline. Spiritual disciplines take sheer determination, but if you determine to circle your children in prayer, you will shape their destinies, just like Susanna Wesley shaped the destinies of her children. Your prayers will live on in their lives long after you die.

Your prayers for your children are the greatest legacy you can leave.

Chapter 2

The *Legend* of the Circle Maker

Truly I tell you, whatever you bind on earth will be bound in heaven, and whatever you loose on earth will be loosed in heaven. Again, truly I tell you that if two of you on earth agree about anything they ask for, it will be done for them by my Father in heaven. For where two or three gather in my name, there am I with them.

MATTHEW 18:18–20

When I discovered the legend of Honi the circle maker in the Jewish Talmud, it changed the way I pray. It gave me a new vocabulary and a new methodology. But before I share the true legend, let me share a word of caution. Every parent has dreams for their children, and if you aren't careful, you'll project your unfulfilled dreams onto your child instead of letting them blaze their own trail.

It's imperative to distinguish between *your will* and *God's will*. Every prayer, including your prayers for your children, must pass a twofold litmus test: your prayers must be *in the will of God* and *for the glory of God.*

God is not a genie in a bottle, and your wish is not His command. His command better be your wish. If it's not, you won't be drawing prayer circles. You'll end up walking in your own circles. So drawing prayer circles starts with discerning what God wants, what God wills.

Prayer is the way we *take our hands off* and *place our children in the hands of God.*

The Legend

For those of you who haven't read *The Circle Maker* yet, let me share the legend behind the book. But instead of the adult version, let me share the version that will soon become a children's book. If you have young children, you might even want to read it to them before dinner or before bed.

> *It had not rained in Israel for one entire year.*
>
> *No clouds in the sky. No water in the well.*

Gardens did not grow. Rivers ran dry. Dust filled the air.

The people were thirsty and scared. They pleaded with one voice, "O God, give us rain!" When God didn't answer right away, some feared He had forgotten them. Then they remembered something, remembered someone.

The rainmaker.

Hardly anyone had seen his face, but nearly everyone had heard his voice. People would travel for days just to hear Honi praying inside his hut on the outskirts of Jerusalem. His aged body was weak, but his childlike faith was strong. His prayers were so powerful that they made people weep.

Like Elijah, who ended a three-year drought with one prayer, Honi was famous for praying for rain. He had the same faith, the same spirit. The people knew that Honi was their last hope, their only hope. So they knocked, and the rainmaker answered.

The people complained, "We can't hear God, and God can't hear us." The rain-

maker replied, "Even if you can't hear God, God can always hear you!" Then he boldly declared, "The same God who made thunder will make it clap. The same God who made the clouds will make them rain."

The parade of people led Honi into the city. As the crowd grew larger, children climbed onto the shoulders of their fathers. Others stood on tiptoe to see what Honi would say, what Honi would do.

That's when it happened.

Honi bowed his head and extended his staff to the ground. "What is he doing?" the people wondered. Then Honi began to turn. He turned all the way around until he stood inside the complete circle he had drawn. Then, with the hope of the entire nation on his shoulders, Honi dropped to his knees. A holy hush came over the crowd so that everyone heard his humble prayer.

"Sovereign Lord, I swear before Your Great Name that I will not leave this circle until you have mercy upon your children."

The words hung in the air. "Is he serious? He won't leave until it rains?" A few *skeptics smirked, but not for long. No one knows whether they felt it or saw it first, but a single raindrop fell from heaven. Then thousands of thirsty souls turned their heads heavenward and caught raindrops in their wide-open mouths. Laughter filled the air. But Honi was still kneeling, still praying.*

"Not for such rain have I prayed, but for rain that will fill cisterns, pits, and caverns."

The sprinkle turned into such a downpour that the crowd fled to higher ground to escape the flash floods. Not Honi. He battled the storm on his knees.

"Not for such rain have I prayed, but for rain of Your favor, blessing, and graciousness."

Then, like a sun shower on a hot summer day, it began to rain calmly, peacefully. Children danced in the downpour like it was the first rainfall they had ever seen, and for some of them, it was.

It was the day thunderclaps applauded God.

It was the day puddle jumping became an act of praise.

It was the day the true legend of the circle maker was born.

Honi the circle maker had taught them the power of prayer. One prayer can change anything. One prayer can change everything. And from that day forth, whenever the people needed a miracle, they would draw a circle and pray just like Honi.

They circled the sick. They circled the sad. They circled the young. They circled the old. They circled their biggest dreams. They circled their greatest fears. And, most importantly, they circled the promises of God.

Sometimes they had to pray for a long, long time. But they never again doubted the fact that God always hears, and God always answers when it is in His will, for His glory. Everyone who witnessed the miracle that day learned a lesson they would never forget: God honors bold prayers because bold prayers honor God.

The Prayer That
Saved a Generation

Some of the members of the Sanhedrin wanted to excommunicate Honi because they believed his prayer was too bold, but it's tough to argue with a miracle. Honi was ultimately honored for "the prayer that saved a generation."

I love that commendation: *the prayer that saved a generation.*

An entire generation of Jews traced their genealogy back to one man, one prayer. Just like Honi, your prayers have the power to save the next generation. You can't choose Christ for your kids, but you can pray that they choose Christ. And I've met far too many children who have come to Christ because their parents prevailed in prayer, sometimes for decades, to believe God for anything less. What other option do we have? To pray or not to pray — these are the only options.

One word of advice to parents of prodigals: form a prayer circle with other parents.

Covenant to pray for each other's children. Why parents? Because no one can pray for children like parents! They have similar heartbreaks, similar hopes. They love their children just like you love yours. Empathy fuels intercession. Just this morning, I was on my knees fighting in prayer for a friend's daughter who is far from God. We need to stand in the gap for one another or, maybe I should say, kneel in the gap.

Your prayers are prophecies. You can write the future of your family with your prayers just like my grandfather did for me. Am I stretching the truth? Not at all. I'm circling the promise in Psalm 103:17:

> But the mercy of the LORD is from
>   everlasting to everlasting
> on those who fear Him,
> and His righteousness to children's
>   children.

Jesus Christ broke the curse of sin at Calvary and secured every spiritual blessing as our inheritance. This is our birthright as children of our heavenly Father, and it is our responsibility as parents to pass down this generational blessing to our earthly children.

Maybe you were the victim of abuse. You didn't have a father or were the child of a divorce. You never felt loved or always felt shamed. And you're afraid you'll make the same mistakes.

Jesus Christ broke the curse so you can break the cycle! This doesn't mean it'll happen quickly or easily. But if you *pray through*, you'll eventually experience the breakthrough. You won't just be blessed; you'll pass on a blessing to the next generation.

Drawing Circles

Since the release of *The Circle Maker*, I've had a steady stream of e-mails and letters from readers who have started circling their dreams, their homes, and their workplaces in prayer. An inner-city teacher circles her classroom every morning, and a realtor circles the properties she represents as listing agent. A team of doctors and nurses circle their patients as they make hospital rounds.

A member of the president's travel pool is circling the White House, and an NFL chaplain is circling his team's practice facility. One reader even circled his bank, praying for a financial miracle — until law enforcement intervened. They thought he was casing it.

There is nothing magical about physically circling something in prayer, but there is something biblical about it. The Israelites circled the city of Jericho until the wall came down. What if they had quit circling after six laps? What if they gave up on the sixth day? They would have forfeited the miracle right before it happened. We tend to give up too quickly, too easily. We need to circle our Jericho until the wall comes tumbling down.

Drawing prayer circles is a metaphor that simply means "to pray without ceasing." It's praying until God answers. It's praying with more intensity, more tenacity. It's not just *praying for*; it's *praying through*. There are times when you have to grab on to the horns of the altar and pray until your knees are numb. We instinctively attach an ASAP to every prayer and ask God to answer *as soon as possible*. We need a paradigm shift. We need to start praying ALAT prayers — *as long as it takes*. That's what praying circles is all about. It's resolving in your heart of hearts that you will pray until the day you die.

Secret Weapon

The most exciting prayer testimonies I've received come from parents who are circling their children in prayer like never before. Parents are praying the promises of God around their children. They are interceding for future spouses, believing for miracles, and praying a hedge of protection around their children. And parents aren't just praying that God will keep their kids safe; they are also praying that He will make them dangerous for His purposes so they can make a difference in their generation. That is the kind of prayer God loves to answer. May God raise up a generation of circle makers who will pray hard, pray bold, and pray through!

One of the most moving testimonies I know of comes from my friend Craig Johnson. Craig and his wife, Samantha, have three children. Their youngest son, Connor, has autism. Like many parents of kids with special needs, Craig and Samantha found themselves teeter-tottering between hope and despair, faith and discouragement. Then they got a copy of *The Circle Maker* and decided it was time to start circling, start believing, start praying again.

Can I come right out and say it? Parenting is the hardest thing you'll ever do. And the more you love your kids, the harder it is. It is spiritually, emotionally, and relationally taxing. And this challenge is multiplied for parents of children with special needs. It takes a heroic effort, and this is exactly what the parents of special needs kids are in my book. Heroes. It takes a special anointing.

Craig and Samantha read about the importance of *praying the Word*, so they decided to circle thirty biblical promises and begin to pray them around Connor. What they didn't know is that Connor was memorizing them — all of them. Without even knowing it, they were planting seeds of faith in his heart. They started by praying these promises before bed at night, and then Connor asked them to pray the promises in the morning too.

Because of his autism, Connor struggles with controlling his emotions, so sometimes he experiences dramatic meltdowns and mood changes. But Connor is now reciting Scripture as a way of helping himself cope. One day, Craig wouldn't let Connor play with his iPad, and Connor quoted from Psalms: "Lord, save me from the pit." Craig and Samantha laughed, and then they cried as they realized that their son was hiding the Word of God in his heart. Another day, Connor cut his foot, and while Samantha put hydrogen peroxide on it, he cried out from James: "Is anyone among you sick? Let him call for the elders of the church, and let them pray over him." Samantha stared in disbelief.

One of the many challenges facing Craig and Samantha is the simple fact that at eight years of age, Connor isn't potty trained. So they decided to circle Connor and pray for a miracle. I'll never forget what Craig said: "Mark, what one person may see as ordinary, another may see as his miracle."

Then Craig told me that not long after they started circling Connor and believing for this miracle, Connor came in from playing outside, and for the first time in his life, went to the bathroom all by himself. Craig started crying as he told me the story; then I started crying. Craig said, "After what seemed like years of drought, God began to send the abundance of rain."

Connor stopped having severe meltdowns. He started eating vegetables and losing some excess weight. Instead of simply repeating everything that was spoken to him, Connor started to respond. And he even tied his own shoelaces for the very first time!

Does this mean the final battle has been fought? We know better; we're parents! The challenges never end, but we need to celebrate our victories along the way. And for the record, prayer is the way we fight our battles. Prayer is the difference between *you fighting for God* and *God fighting for you.*

Secret prayer is our secret weapon.

When we get on our knees, God extends His powerful right hand on our behalf.

For the record, Craig and Samantha aren't just circling their own children; they are promoting a cause by starting Champions Clubs and Champions Academies (development centers and charter schools) that will serve children with special needs all across the country.

The earth has circled the sun more than two thousand times since the day Honi drew his circle in the sand, but God is still looking for circle makers. He is still looking for those who dream big and pray hard.

It starts with our family circle!

Chapter 3

Five

Prayer Circles

Rise during the night and cry out.
  Pour out your hearts like water to the Lord.
Lift up your hands to him in prayer,
  pleading for your children.

LAMENTATIONS 2:19 NLT

Let me formally introduce you to my wife and three children.

Lora and I are high school sweethearts. We dated all the way through college and got married two weeks after graduation. We have been happily married for eighteen years, and we'll celebrate our twentieth anniversary later this year. Yes, you read that right. The first two years were rough sailing. We were both very young and very stubborn, but we weathered the storm, and it's those tough times that have helped us appreciate the good times.

Lora and I decided to start our family young. It felt like we were kids when we had our kids. We were high on energy and low on wisdom. Sixteen years and three children later, we have a little more wisdom and a lot less energy!

Our oldest son, Parker, is now sixteen. Summer Joy is fourteen going on seventeen. And Josiah just turned ten.

I honestly thought we'd have more children when we got married. I wanted five kids so we could field a complete basketball team, but a near-death experience between our second and third child interrupted our family planning. So three it was, and three it is. I like to describe it this way: our energy is divided by three, but our joy is multiplied by three.

For the record, I don't love my kids equally. No parent does. I love them uniquely. Their passions and personalities couldn't be more different, which means we had to learn how to parent all over again with each of them. They respond to discipline very differently, and they speak different love languages.

I have come to terms with the fact that I've done more things wrong than I've done right as a parent, but I've taken courage from this simple truth: it's not just my wife and I who are raising our kids; we have a heavenly Father who compensates for our deficiencies, weaknesses, and mistakes. Where we fail as earthly parents, I believe our heavenly Father can succeed.

Parent or Prophet?

If you asked me what I pray for as a parent more than anything else, the answer is the favor of God. While it's difficult to describe or define, *the favor of God is what God can do for you that you cannot do for yourself.*

When Parker was a baby, I circled Luke 2:52 and turned it into a prayer blessing. I have prayed this blessing around each of my children thousands of times. Almost every night when they were young, I tucked them into bed with this simple prayer: *Lord, let them grow in wisdom and stature, and in favor with God and man.*

I realize that Luke 2:52 isn't technically a promise, but I think I'm on sound theological ground. This one verse is a time-lapse of Jesus' development as a child, and we're called to be just like Jesus, so why wouldn't I circle it? Why shouldn't I turn it into a blessing and pray it around my children?

Please listen to me, parents: *you are prophets to your children.*

Jewish philosophers did not believe the prophetic gift was reserved for a few select individuals. They believed that becoming prophetic was the crowning point of mental and spiritual development. It was the natural by-product of spiritual development. The more one grows in grace, the more prophetic one becomes.

This doesn't mean you will start predicting the future. It means you'll start creating it. How? Through your prayers! Prayer is the way we write the future. It's the difference between *letting things happen* and *making things happen.*

Personal Prophecies

I once read that at least 40 percent of our lives are based on personal prophecies. I'm not sure how you substantiate a statistic like that, but I find it very believable. The right word spoken at the right time can make an eternal difference.

We all need personal prophets in our lives. And I pray that my children encounter a lot of people who have a profound positive influence on their lives. Right at the top of the list are the unsung heroes of the kingdom — youth pastors. I'm deeply grateful for youth pastors to tag-team with me as a parent, but let me make one thing clear: it's not their responsibility to disciple my children. That's my responsibility! You cannot delegate discipleship any more than you can delegate prayer.

You need to speak words of comfort and encouragement to your children. When you catch them doing something wrong, gently rebuke them. Lovingly remind them: *that's not who you are*. When you catch them doing something right, reinforce it. Fan into flame the gift of God that is in them.

In the pages that follow, I want to share five biblical and practical ways to circle your kids in prayer. But before we start circling, let me share a few guidelines. First, you don't have to do all five simultaneously. In fact, I encourage you to focus on one or two of them at a time. Second, you won't master these approaches to prayer right away. Prayer takes practice, and practice makes perfect. But if you stick with it, these prayer habits will become second nature. Finally, ask the Holy Spirit to give you your own ideas. Don't just adopt these habits; adapt them to your unique situation, your unique personality.

Let's draw the first circle.

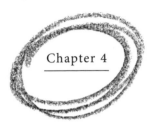

Chapter 4

The 1st Circle: Circling the *Promises* of God

*For no matter how many
promises God has made,
they are "Yes" in Christ.*

2 CORINTHIANS 1:20

One of your chief responsibilities as a parent is to be a student of your child. You aren't just a prophet who speaks into their future; you are also a historian who records their past. In one sense, you know your children better than they know themselves. They can't remember their first few years of life; you cannot forget. You remember their first words, their first steps, and their first day of school like it was yesterday.

You have a unique vantage point as a parent. No one sees the past, present, and future quite like you do. It's your job to help your children connect the dots between who they were, who they are, and who they are becoming.

As long as we are clothed in flesh, we're unable to see the majesty and mystery of who we truly are. Our true identity will only be revealed on the day our heavenly Father calls us by our new name. Until then, we have to use the name given to us by our earthly parents. We also have to rely on our earthly parents to help us discover who we are.

Part of your role as prophet-historian is to *know your children* and *know Scripture* so you can train them in the way they should go. When children enter a new season of life, it is full of uncertainties and insecurities. Our kids can experience an identity crisis because they aren't sure where they fit or who they are. When they enter middle school or high school or college, we need to intercede for our children. Pray that they will make the right friends and the right choices. Pray that their conscience will keep them on the straight and narrow. Pray that they won't just survive; pray that they will thrive.

If your kids have a difficult time discerning or doing the will of God, you may even have to agonize in prayer for them like Jesus did in Gethsemane. This kind of prayer is part of parenting. You've got to pray the price — and the price is blood, sweat, and tears.

Holy Confidence

I spent several agonizing hours interceding for Summer recently as she made what I felt was a critical decision. She had decided to try out for her freshman volleyball team, even though she had never played organized volleyball before. I felt added responsibility because she did so with my strong encouragement. On the first day of tryouts, all four grades played together and she felt overwhelmed by the talent level of some of the seniors who were NCAA Division 1 – caliber players. Summer decided to quit after the first day, but I felt she should stick with it. I didn't want her first experience with high school to be dropping out of a tryout, but I also empathized with her. To make matters worse, I wasn't home because I was hiking Half Dome in Yosemite National Park with Parker.

I was on the phone with Summer and Lora quite a bit that night. I didn't know what to do or what to say, but I knew we needed to pray. Our hike was scheduled to start before sunrise the next morning, but I couldn't sleep. I spent several hours in the shadow of Half Dome praying that God would give Summer the courage she needed to keep going. I also prayed that something would happen to change her mind, but I had no idea what that might be. The next day, the varsity volleyball coach called our house. Are you kidding me? He didn't have to do that. I honestly couldn't believe it. Well, that phone call was the catalyst that got Summer to go back and try out. I was so proud of her! And I wasn't proud just because she made the team and had a great season; I was proud because she swallowed her pride, faced her fears, and took a risk.

I know this situation may not sound significant to you, and it certainly wasn't a matter of life or death, but I just felt in my spirit that it would set an important precedent in Summer's life. This was the kind of thing that could either give her confidence or rob her of confidence.

Since that night of intercession, one of my recurrent prayers for Summer is that she will grow in confidence. I'm not talking about self-confidence. I'm praying for *holy confidence* that comes from doing the will of God for the glory of God. It's a confidence that is anchored in the power of God, the grace of God, and the word of God. So over the next several months, I searched for any and every verse of Scripture that spoke of confidence, and I read those passages to Summer before school during our ten-minute devotional time. I wanted these promises to get into her spirit, into her subconscious.

The Peace That
Transcends Understanding

Josiah is at a very different age and stage. Most of our prayers revolve around his fears. These fears can be frustrating at times, but patience is the by-product of remembering some of our own childhood challenges.

For me, the big one was Big Foot. I was convinced he lived under my bed or in my closet, and my brother didn't help matters. Our family tradition was saying good night from our respective rooms, so I would yell into the darkness, "Good night, Mom. Good night, Dad. Good night, Don." My brother would respond, "Good night, Mom. Good night, Dad. Good night, Mark. Good night, Big Foot." Got me every time! My mom and dad would have to get up and redo the closet check and bed check.

Now here's the thing: my fear was totally irrational. If Big Foot could fit in my closet or under my bed, he wasn't really that big! But you cannot reason with irrational fears. *Irrational fears only submit to prayer.*

Our most powerful prayers are hyper-linked to the promises of God. One of my favorites is found in Philippians 4:6 – 7:

> Do not be anxious about anything, but in every situation, by prayer and petition, with thanksgiving, present your requests to God. And the peace of God, which transcends all understanding, will guard your hearts and your minds in Christ Jesus.

I'm praying this promise, and Josiah is memorizing it. He is learning that when we circle the promises of God, those promises then encircle us. The peace that transcends understanding literally guards our hearts and minds.

Love Girls

One of the promises that God put into my heart for Parker is that he will grow up to *love God* and *love girls*. The first one is obvious. I'm praying that he is great at the Great Commandment. I'm praying that he'll love

God with all his heart and soul and mind and strength.

Let me explain the second one: *love girls.*

We live in a culture full of sexual brokenness, and I think it's the by-product of sexual confusion. Part of the problem is that churches are answering the questions no one is asking instead of talking about what everybody is thinking about. Sex is at the top of the list.

One of our sacred responsibilities is to teach our kids the difference between right and wrong, and nowhere is this more necessary than our approach to the topic of sexuality. We need to celebrate sex as a gift from God. Sex is not just a good thing; it's a God thing. We also need to help our children understand that sex is intended for the enjoyment of a husband and wife in the context of marriage. Sex outside the marriage covenant is sin. Our culture today tells us it's wrong to say something is wrong, and I think that's wrong. If we don't use our voice, we lose our voice.

Now here's my advice when it comes to

teaching our kids about sexuality: *Don't just say it; pray it.* You've got to have "the talk." But you also need to circle Psalm 37:4:

> Delight yourself in the LORD;
> > And He will give you the desires
> > of your heart.

This promise doesn't mean that God will give you whatever you want. Quite the contrary! It means that if you genuinely delight yourself in the Lord, then the Spirit of God will radically change your desires. There is no doubt that old desires die hard — they seem to have nine lives. But dying to self means dying to our sinful desires. And the Holy Spirit will conceive new desires, holy desires, within you.

So don't just pray that your teenager doesn't get pregnant; pray that she gets pregnant with the Holy Spirit. Don't just pray defensively that your child won't do anything wrong; pray that they'll do something right.

When you pray the word of God, it's like downloading updates to your operating system. You continually upgrade your conscience so it is fine-tuned to the Holy Spirit and the Holy Scriptures.

Keep Circling

Even when things look hopeless and you feel helpless, you need to keep circling the promises of God. I'm not saying that God will override the free will of our children, but He can do a miracle in their hearts.

During one of my stops on *The Circle Maker* book tour, I met a husband and wife who were heartbroken because of a broken relationship with their son. When he told them he was gay, they didn't know how to respond. Both sides made some mistakes and said some things they regretted. It had been a decade since they had last talked to him, and their sadness was deep.

When they heard the legend of Honi the circle maker, they felt it was time to start circling again. We actually held hands and formed a prayer circle on the spot. Less than a month later, their prodigal son came home.

Is there a lot of healing that must still take

place? Absolutely. You don't solve ten years of problems in ten minutes or ten days. I'm not saying that God cannot bring immediate healing or instantaneous deliverance, but we often have to get out of problems the way we got into them — one step at a time. Prayer is the first step. And that one small step can turn into a giant leap.

Chapter 5

The 2nd Circle: *Making* Prayer Lists

*Listen to my voice in the morning, LORD.
Each morning I bring my requests to you
and wait expectantly.*

PSALM 5:3 NLT

I'm the worst grocery shopper in the world. I rarely bring home everything I was supposed to get, and I always bring home something I shouldn't have gotten. Why? Probably because I don't shop with a grocery list. Evidently I'm not alone, because supermarket studies have found that while nearly 100 percent of women come armed with a shopping list, less than 25 percent of men carry a list. Between 60 to 70 percent of all grocery purchases made by men are unplanned. The study did show one area, however, in which men outshop women — junk food. Hail to the male gender!

I know that making lists isn't part of everybody's personality, and making lists doesn't sound very exciting, but is there a better way to make sure we do what needs to be done? And if we need a grocery list, an invite list, and a to-do list, is it possible we need a prayer list?

The goal of a prayer list is not to lay out a laundry list before God. In fact, prayer is not about our agenda for God at all; it's about discovering God's agenda for us. But once we discover His agenda, we have to write it down. In my experience, it's very difficult to pray with specificity, intentionality, and consistency without a prayer list. And for the record, I encourage you to keep a record. Then you can give God the glory when He answers your prayers.

Prayer Journal

At the beginning of this year, Lora and I spent one of our coffee dates making a prayer list for our children. Some of these prayers are probably prayers that every parent prays for their children, but we also tried to personalize our list based on the unique personalities and passions of our children.

One of the prayers that made the list is this: *Lord, let their ears be tuned to the still small voice of the Holy Spirit.* I want my children to *find their voice*, and the key is *hearing the voice of God.* If they don't hear the voice of God, they will echo our culture. But if they listen to God, people will listen to them and they'll become a voice to their generation. I want my children to have a prophetic voice, but it starts with having a prophetic ear. So I am specifically praying that God will give them the ear of Samuel.

I can't wait to show my children the prayers I have journaled for them. Some of them I have already revealed, but some I won't share until those prayers are answered. One way or the other, you need to document your prayers by writing them in a prayer journal. Journal like a journalist, because that's what you are to your children.

I have a friend whose father journaled prayers for her and her two sisters without them even knowing it. In fact, my friend didn't find out until after her father died. This journal is one of her treasured possessions. Imagine being able to go back and see what your parents were praying for you two or twelve or twenty years ago. One thing is certain: it would enable them to give God the praise He deserves for the prayers He has answered.

Prayer Posters

A few years ago, our friends Dennis and Donna, who pastor a neighboring church on Capitol Hill, told us about something God had impressed on them to do for their children. They identified words that were *descriptive* and *prescriptive* of their kids, had these words framed, and hung them on the walls in their rooms. They often wondered whether those words meant anything, but their oldest daughter, who is grown-up and no longer in their home, recently told them that some nights, when she hadn't been able to fall asleep, she would look at those words on the wall and they would speak to her. Those framed words started to frame her. She started to see herself in the light of her God-ordained identity and destiny.

Lora and I loved the idea so much that we adapted it for Summer. Prior to Summer's thirteenth birthday, Lora recruited two of Summer's aunts to help her come up with a list of prophetic words to speak into Summer's life. Each of them took three words and discussed them over a special birthday dinner. Then we had a graphic designer turn those nine words into a poster. Each word is rendered in a different font, and these different fonts represent nine different dimensions of her identity, her destiny. These nine words are nine prayers that we'll pray for Summer for the rest of her life. It's a prayer list with a creative twist. Sometimes I'll go into Summer's room and use the poster as my prayer list. I also have a picture of it on my phone.

Lunch Box Notes

Our friends Brad and Angie developed an interesting adaptation of this idea that they call lunch box notes. Like many parents, Angie dreaded the daily drudgery of packing brown-bag lunches for their three kids, so she decided to redeem the task. At first she looked for notes from Hallmark, but all she found was "You're a rock star" or "You're the coolest cat in class."

Angie decided to buy a pack of sticky notes and started writing Scriptures and promises and prayers. If one of the kids had an exam, she would circle a Scripture like Psalm 121: "My help comes from the LORD." Sometimes she wrote down a challenge: if you see someone in need, be the first person to help.

One of the keys to prayer is speaking in the language your kids understand. If their native tongue is texting, then you need to send texts at different times of the day, letting them know you are circling them in prayer. But no matter what medium you use, praying circles around your children begins by identifying and specifying the promises you are believing God for.

A Book of Prayers

A few years ago, one of our campus pastors came up with what I thought was a brilliant idea. I'm not sure where it originated, but Chris and Lora asked family and friends to write out a prayer for their first son, Torin. They did the same thing for their second son, Declan. Then they bound that collection of prayers together and created a prayer book.

I can only imagine the moment when Chris and Lora give the prayer books to their sons. Seeing the prayers that were prayed for them before they were even born will flood their hearts with awe at the faithfulness of God.

I love the idea of putting together a prayer book before a baby is even born, but it's never too late. You can do it before the first day of kindergarten or after the last day of high school. You can even make it a wedding gift.

Chapter 6

The 3rd Circle:
Creating Prayer
Mantras

*"When you pray, don't babble on and
on as people of other religions do."*

MATTHEW 6:7 NLT

As you read through the Bible, certain words, phrases, or verses will jump off the page and into your spirit. The ones you circle over and over again will become prayer mantras.

Over the years, our family has adopted a handful of mantras from a wide variety of sources. One of the most commonly quoted is this: *Your focus determines your reality*. That's what Qui-Gon Jinn said to Anakin Skywalker in *Star Wars: Episode I – The Phantom Menace*. Whenever one of us is in a funk, we'll pull out this mantra and try to refocus on things that are true, noble, right, and pure, a la Philippians 4:8. One of my favorite mantras is a deep thought by Jack Handey: *If you ever drop your keys into a river of molten lava, let 'em go, because, man, they're gone.* I don't even have to quote the whole thing anymore. All I have to say is, "If you ever drop your keys ..." It's a reminder to let go and let God.

We have a natural tendency to *remember what we should forget* and *forget what we should remember*. That's where mantras come in. They serve as reminders of *who we are* and *what we're about* as a family. And there is something about repeating them consistently that gets them from the head to the heart. They become part of our operating system.

There is something powerful about a single God-inspired prayer repeated throughout a child's lifetime. I like to call it a prayer mantra. I've already mentioned a few of my prayer mantras, but the most significant one is Luke 2:52: *May you grow in wisdom and stature, and in favor with God and man.*

Not long ago, Josiah came home from school super excited. He said, "Dad, you know that verse you pray for me every day? We read it in school today." He was beaming from ear to ear. It made my day because I could tell that the promise we've circled thousands of times is hardwired into his heart.

Do I ever give this prayer mantra new language? Yes. I pray for favor in the classroom and favor on the court. I pray for favor when they are applying for jobs or applying for schools. I pray that God will anoint their right brains and give them God ideas. I pray that God will open doors of opportunity. So I pray in lots of different ways, but more often than not, I repeat the same prayer mantra so it gets engraved on their souls.

So how do you get started? Here are a few simple ideas.

First of all, *pray about what to pray about*. This is the first object of prayer. The purpose of prayer is not to outline *our agenda* for God; the purpose is to get into the presence of God and get *God's agenda* for us.

Second, you need to go back to the Bible. And don't just read it. If all you do is read the Bible, then you are actually *mis*reading it. The Bible wasn't meant to be read; it was meant to be prayed. Start reading, and God will start speaking. And that's when you need to stop reading and start praying.

A King, a Proverbs 31 Woman, and a Cheerful and Obedient Boy

Remember when Samuel went out looking for the next king of Israel, and David's father, Jesse, didn't even bother to call David in from the fields? David's own dad didn't see who he could or would become. When Jesse looked at David, he saw a shepherd boy; when Samuel looked at David, he saw a king. One of the great dangers of family relationships is that we become blind to beauty and mystery simply because we live in such close proximity.

You need a vision for your children.

With your physical eyes you *see who a*

person is. With your spiritual eyes you *see what that person can be.* And it's only when you close your physical eyes in prayer that God will open your spiritual eyes to perceive what is far more real than the reality you can perceive with your five senses.

One reader of *The Circle Maker* wrote to tell me that he is praying that his two daughters become Proverbs 31 women. When he first started praying this prayer, his oldest daughter asked him what it meant. He told her to read this passage, pray it, and study it. As she does, she is discovering her destiny. Proverbs 31 is the mirror that enables her to see who she really is in Christ.

One night, while he was praying for his daughters, he forgot to include his prayer mantra. His youngest daughter reminded him, "Daddy, you forgot to say that we would be Proverbs 31 women." That's when you know the prayer mantra is working!

I got another e-mail from a reader who echoes the same prayer day in and day out. His son wasn't inherently cheerful or obedient by nature, but that is what he felt led to pray for. His prayer mantra? That his son would be *cheerful and obedient*. After years of praying this prophetic prayer, this man has seen his son's disposition change and new tendencies and capacities created within his son.

Life Themes

Every life is comprised of a few themes.

One of our primary responsibilities as parents is helping our children identify their life themes. We need to help them find the sweet spot where their God-given gifts and God-ordained passions overlap.

One of my professors in graduate school put it this way: *What makes you cry or pound your fist on the table?* In other words, "What makes you sad or mad?" I would add *glad* to the mix.

In the words of Frederick Buechner, "The voice we should listen to most as we choose a vocation is the voice that we might think we should listen to least, and that is the voice of our own gladness. What can we do that makes us the gladdest, what can we do that leaves us with the strongest sense of sailing true north and of peace, which is much of what gladness is?... I believe that if it is a thing that makes us truly glad, then it is a good thing and it is our thing."

What makes our kids laugh? What makes them cry? What gets them upset? If we want to discover their destinies, we need to follow their trails of tears, their clenched fists, and their smiles.

As God reveals these life themes, you may want to consider coupling them with a life verse. I don't think you want to do this lightly. And I'm certainly not suggesting that you emphasize one verse to the exclusion of others. But God will give you different verses for different seasons or verses that complement each other. You may find yourself praying for your child to be "strong and courageous" or to do "what is right in the eyes of the Lord." I find myself praying these two biblical mantras for Josiah all the time.

A number of readers have shared with

me the life verses they have prayed for their children for ten or twenty or thirty years. It's amazing how often these life verses become life themes!

Chapter 7

The 4th Circle:
Forming
Prayer Circles

Don't let anyone look down on you because you are young, but set an example for the believers in speech, in conduct, in love, in faith and in purity.

1 TIMOTHY 4:12

A few years ago, as our family was having devotions, I felt prompted to circle Josiah and pray for him. I put my hands on his chest and prayed for my son. Actually, I felt like I was praying *into* him. It was like the physical contact created a conduit between my son and me. It's not like there was anything magical about it, but there was something biblical about it.

I felt like the Holy Spirit put a prayer in my heart so I boldly declared it: *Lord,*

let Josiah grow into the destiny of his name.
As you may have guessed, Josiah is named
after an ancient Jewish king whose spiritual
exploits were many but are summarized in
one mantra: *He did what was right in the eyes
of the Lord.* I was declaring Josiah's destiny.

Later that night, after brushing his teeth
and putting on his pajamas, Josiah inno-
cently said, "Dad, I can't wait to grow up to
be a king." Slight misinterpretation of my
prayer! Lora asked me if I corrected him.
Nope. Didn't have the heart.

Then Josiah said something that helped
me appreciate an ancient biblical ritual in a
way that no theologian could teach. He said,
"Dad, have you done that hands things with
Parker and Summer?" Josiah didn't have the
theological terminology down pat or fully
understand the biblical precedent, but he
thought the laying on of hands was the coolest thing in the world. And it is. But it's more
than that. It creates a prayer bond between
parent and child.

The Laying on of Hands

Do you remember when parents brought their children to be blessed by Jesus? Jesus didn't just pronounce a blessing over their lives; he put his hands on their heads. Why wouldn't we follow suit?

Research has shown that touch has the power to fight viruses, relieve stress, improve sleep, and help us recover more quickly from injury. One study done by a group of Utah researchers found that a thirty-minute massage three times a week lowers levels of the stress-related enzyme alpha-amylase by 34 percent. You may want to underline this last sentence and put it on your spouse's nightstand.

The power of touch, even on a human level, is an amazing thing. But when you add the power of God to the equation, it sets the stage for something supernatural. The biblical practice of the laying on of hands is an endangered practice in many church circles. We don't do it for a wide range of reasons. Maybe the church you grew up in didn't do it, or it feels a little too close for comfort. Whatever the reason, the net result can be a lack of faith, a lack of miracles, a lack of deliverance.

Call me a simpleton, but I believe that if we simply do what the people in the Bible did, we may experience what they experienced. Who knows how many miraculous moments we've forfeited because we've failed to act in a bold biblical fashion by praying for someone who is sick, commissioning someone who is called, or encouraging someone who just needs a hand on his or her shoulder? And it ought to start in the home with our children.

Praying With versus Praying For

One reason I love the story of King Josiah is that he was only eight years old when he assumed the throne

Age is never an excuse.

You're never too young or too old to be used by God. King Josiah didn't let his youthfulness keep him from calling a nation to bend its knees. Whatever you do, don't underestimate your children's potential. Give them opportunities to exercise their spiritual gifts, and they might just surprise you.

Great parenting doesn't just mean *teaching your kids*; it also means *learning from them*. Think of it as reverse mentoring. After all, Jesus said, "Unless you change and become like little children, you will never enter the kingdom of heaven."

When I'm in a place of spiritual desperation, I often ask my kids to pray. There is something uniquely powerful about children's prayers — and it's their childlike faith. Their faith hasn't been infected by logic yet. In *The Circle Maker*, I shared the story of an eight million dollar piece of property on Capitol Hill that we own debt free. It took a miracle to get a contract on it, and I believe the genesis of that miracle was a simple prayer prayed by one of my children.

On the very day we thought we would sign a contract on that property, we lost the contract to a real estate development corporation. I felt defeated. I went home and asked our family to kneel in prayer. I had lost faith, but my kids had not. I'll never forget one of the prayers: "God, use that property for your glory." It was so simple. It was so pure. It was so full of faith. Somehow that prayer resuscitated my faith, and I knew God would answer.

Backseat versus Driver's Seat

The day I turned sixteen, I went to the local Department of Motor Vehicles to get my license. I couldn't wait. I'll never forget the feeling of freedom as I sat behind the wheel for the first time. *I can go anywhere I want*, but then it dawned on me as I approached the end of our block, *I don't know how to get anywhere*. I had a newfound freedom but no sense of the direction. The crazy thing is that I had crisscrossed every square inch of my hometown — Naperville, Illinois — a thousand times. Why did I suddenly not know where to drive? Because I had been in the backseat, not the driver's seat. I hadn't been paying attention to where we were going or how we got there. I was just along for the ride.

The same is true spiritually. Until kids get into the driver's seat, they won't know how to get anywhere. What do I mean? You can pray *for* them their entire lives, but if you never let them pray, they're just along for the ride. They won't know how to get anywhere in prayer.

One of the greatest responsibilities of parenthood is praying for your kids, but an even greater responsibility is teaching your kids to pray. Don't just pray *for* them; pray *with* them. Praying *for* your kids is like taking them for a ride; praying *with* your kids is like teaching them to drive. If all you ever do is pray *for* your kids, they'll just stay in the backseat. Your kids will become spiritual codependents who ask you for a ride anytime they need to get somewhere spiritually. But if you teach them to pray, they can download directions themselves and make their way to wherever it is that God wants them to go.

You can't practice the spiritual disciplines *for* your kids; you have to practice them *with* your kids. Last year for Lent, Parker and I did a little prayer experiment, or as I like to call it, an experiLent. We decided to get up at six o' clock on school days to give us a little extra time to pray together in the morning. We decided we would kneel in prayer. Then we took turns praying for each other. Was every prayer time amazing? No. In fact, I had to nudge Parker a time or two because my prayer put him to sleep! But we also had some powerful times kneeling in the presence of God before his throne. I'm not sure I can teach my children anything more important or more powerful than kneeling before God in prayer.

Aaron and Hur

After *The Circle Maker* released, I embarked on a book tour that took me to a dozen cities in the span of ten weeks. I love book tours because I love connecting with readers in person, but these tours also take a toll.

During that book tour, National Community Church was going through a significant growth spurt that demanded every ounce of creativity and energy I had. So between the speaking and pastoring, I was pretty well spent.

Right before one of those trips, I asked my family to pray for me. I'm usually on the praying end, but I needed to be on the receiving end. So I knelt down, and my wife and children laid hands on me. They took turns praying for me, and as they prayed, I could hardly keep from crying. I felt so loved, so empowered, so encouraged by that prayer circle. Then, when everyone had taken their turn and I thought they were done, Parker started praying again. This was no perfunctory prayer. I could tell the Holy Spirit had inspired him to add something to his earlier prayer. He put his hand on my back and prayed, "Lord, I pray that Pops would maintain his integrity and transparency during this stressful season."

When your own son prays that kind of prayer for you, it takes accountability to a whole new level. It was like the Holy Spirit steeled my resolve to live with integrity and transparency.

Remember the story of Aaron and Hur holding up the arms of Moses during battle? Moses had lost his strength, and when he lowered his arms, the Israelite army lost ground. But as long as Aaron and Hur lifted his arms, the army was victorious.

All of us need Aarons and Hurs in our lives. We need people who are strong when we're weak. We need people who are full of faith when we're running on empty. We need people who will fight for us on their knees. We all need a prayer circle!

Sometimes parents play the role of Aaron and Hur, but sometimes our children hold up our arms. I recently got an e-mail from a dad who had been unemployed for eight long months. He was angry with God and angry with himself. He had stopped leading family devotions because he felt like a failure on the job front. After reading *The Circle Maker*, he decided it was time to start again. He led his family in prayer for the first time in a long time. Then his wife and kids prayed for him. As his wife prayed, his children literally held up his arms, just like Aaron and Hur did for Moses.

It was a moment he'll never forget.

That's what families are for.

Chapter 8

The 5th Circle: *Praying* through the Bible

As the rain and the snow
  come down from heaven,
and do not return to it
  without watering the earth
and making it bud and flourish,
  so that it yields seed for the sower and
    bread for the eater,
so is my word that goes out from my mouth:
  It will not return to me empty,
but will accomplish what I desire
  and achieve the purpose for which I sent it.

ISAIAH 55:10–11

One of my most treasured possessions is a Bible that belonged to my Grandpa Johnson. I love seeing his notes in the margins. I love seeing which verses he underlined. Sometimes I'll even do personal devotions out of his Bible.

I want to leave a similar legacy for my children. In fact, I want to give each of my children a Bible that was prayed through specifically for them. I recently got my hands on a Bible edition inspired by an idea that comes from Jonathan Edwards, the eighteenth-century theologian and pastor.

Edwards loved writing notes while he read, so he hand-stitched blank pages into his Bible. In the Bible edition I have, every other page is blank, allowing me to write prayers and record thoughts for my children. I'll give each of them their own personal copy before they go off to college.

My friend Wayne has done the same thing for his children. He prayed through the entire Bible with each of his children in mind, starting with his oldest son, Timothy. He circled and underlined verses that were Timothy-specific. He wrote notes in the margins. He literally prayed every promise for his children.

Then a few weeks before Timothy graduated from high school, Wayne planned a special event at a nearby restaurant — all of which was a complete surprise to his son. A handful of influencers in Timothy's life presented him with gifts. Wayne gave him the "finisher" medal from his third Marine Corps Marathon. But the most significant moment, and the most significant gift, came when Wayne gave Timothy the Bible. In

Wayne's words, "My greatest joy is knowing I have prayed every word of God, every promise of God, with Timothy in mind." Wayne said it was one of the few times in his life when he saw grown men sobbing uncontrollably.

Now let's be honest, our children don't always appreciate what we do for them at the moment when we do it. It's usually not until we have kids of our own that we appreciate the sacrifices our parents made. So don't be disappointed if you feel your prayer circles aren't making a difference. They are. They will. Or maybe you feel it's too little too late. Listen, it's never too late to be who you might have been. Maybe your kids are already adults and you feel like you missed your opportunity. God gives us a second chance, and it's called *becoming a grandparent*. You can do for your grandchildren what you failed to do for your children.

Live Unoffended

My friends John and Heidi are part of my personal prayer circle, and God has given them some amazing answers to the prayers they've prayed for others, but many of their prayers for their own family have gone unanswered. A step of faith into the world of filmmaking resulted in the loss of their life savings when financial backing didn't materialize as promised. Their family had to move out of their home because of a fire. They lost three of four parents in four years. And a rare genetic condition has taken a toll physically, emotionally, and financially. It almost seems as though God answers every prayer they pray *except* the prayers they pray for their own family.

There have been moments when they've been tempted to throw in the prayer towel. But one promise has sustained them through the toughest times: *Blessed is the one who is not offended by me.*

Here's the context of this promise.

Jesus is doing miracles right and left. He

is healing diseases, driving out demons, and restoring sight to the blind, but John the Baptist misses the miracle train. It seems like Jesus is rescuing everybody except his most faithful follower, who is in prison. And John is his cousin! It seems that Jesus could have, and maybe should have, organized a rescue operation and busted him out before John was beheaded. Instead Jesus sends a message via John's disciples. He tells them to tell John about all the miracles Jesus is doing and then he asks them to relay this promise: *Blessed is the one who is not offended by me.*

Have you ever felt that God was doing miracles for everyone and their brother, but you seem to be the odd one out? That God seems to be keeping His promises to everyone but you and your family? I wonder if that's how John the Baptist felt. And don't forget, he was family.

So what do you do when you feel like God is answering everyone's prayers but yours? In the words of my friends, who have experienced their fair share of unanswered prayers, "We try to live our lives unoffended by God. Jesus promises blessing if we are not offended when He does things for others. And if He does it for them, He might do it for us. We don't know why God does what He does. We do know that 100 percent of the prayers we don't pray won't get answered."

I love this approach to prayer, this approach to life. It's the circle maker's mantra: *100 percent of the prayers I don't pray won't get answered.*

Hyperlinked

One of the challenges John and Heidi have faced as they try to live unoffended by God involves their son. He was a normally developing toddler until one day when he suddenly and mysteriously lost all communication. They wondered if he would ever talk again. The fear of a wide variety of diagnoses, including high functioning autism, dropped them to their knees.

During those desperate days, they went to visit their pastor for counsel and encouragement. While praying for them, God gave him a promise. He jotted Isaiah 59:21 on a sticky note and handed it to them.

"As for me, this is my covenant with them," says the LORD. "My Spirit, who is on you, will not depart from you, and my words that I have put in your mouth will always be on your lips, on the lips of your children and on the lips of their descendants — from this time on and forever," says the LORD.

The pastor shut his Bible and said, "I guess that settles it. Your child will talk."

For the past ten years, their prayers have been hyperlinked to that promise. In that moment, John and Heidi said "a wall came crashing down" and "a promise came rushing in." It was the most naturally supernatural moment of their lives. Has it been clear sailing since then? No. Have they experienced disappointments? Yes. But that promise is circled in their Bible. "God gave us a promise, and no matter how many times we have to keep circling, it's settled."

The other night, Lora and I had dinner

with John and Heidi. The highlight? When they told us their son brought home a 4.0 GPA on his most recent report card. I've been rejoicing ever since, and I absolutely believe that his academic performance is directly linked to the biblical promise his parents have circled for more than a decade.

Chapter 9

~~Holy~~ Complications

Children are a gift from the Lord;
*   they are a reward from him.*
Children born to a young man
*   are like arrows in a warrior's hands.*

PSALM 127:3–4 NLT

One reason many people get frustrated spiritually is that they believe it should get easier to do the will of God. I don't know if my comment here will be encouraging or discouraging, but the will of God doesn't get easier; it gets harder. It doesn't get less complicated; it gets more complicated. But I believe these complications are evidence of God's blessing. And if a complication is from God, then it's a holy complication.

You need to come to terms with this two-sided truth: *The blessings of God won't just bless you; they will also complicate your life.* Sin will complicate your life in negative ways, in ways it should not be complicated; the blessings of God will complicate your life in positive ways, in ways it should be complicated.

When Lora and I got married, it complicated our lives. Praise God for complications! We have three complications named Parker, Summer, and Josiah. I can't imagine my life without these complications. With every promotion, there are complications. As you earn more income, your taxes will become more complicated. My point? Blessings will complicate your life, but they will complicate your life in the way God wants.

So my prayer for myself — and for you — is this: *Lord, complicate our lives.*

Sleepless Nights

Some of the longest nights of my life were the sleepless nights when Parker was a baby. He had a bad case of colic that caused him to cry incessantly for no discernible reason. The joy of having our first child was quickly displaced by sleep deprivation. The only thing that would calm his crying was running the bathtub. I remember going into the bathroom, turning on the faucet, and holding him for hours on end. Our water bill was so uncharacteristically high that the water company actually thought there had been some kind of mistake. Nope. Just a crying baby!

When you're holding a baby who won't stop crying, you can't stop praying. It's all we knew to do. Parker must be one of the most prayed-for babies in his generation. That's the reason I'm grateful for his colic. That's the reason I believe God will use him in great ways. We wrapped our arms around him and prayed circles around him every time he cried. Those were some long nights and long prayers, but now that we're seeing these prayers answered in his life as a teenager, we wouldn't trade those sleepless nights for anything in the world.

When we get discouraged as parents, we have to remember the power of a single prayer. One prayer can change anything, change everything. This I know from personal experience.

On Call

Our family started attending Calvary Church when I was in the eighth grade. It was already a megachurch with thousands of members, but my father-in-law had an amazing memory for names and faces. If he met you once, he would remember your name forever. Despite the size of the church, he had a hospitable spirit that gave him an air of accessibility. Maybe that's why my parents felt like they could call him at two o'clock in the morning after my doctor issued a code blue and half a dozen nurses came rushing into my ICU room. I thought I was taking my last breath.

My mom stayed by my side while my dad called information and got a home phone number for the Schmidgalls. In less than ten minutes, my future father-in-law was at my bedside in his black double-breasted superman suit that I would later swear he slept in.

My father-in-law was a large man with large hands. They looked more like meat hooks than hands. When he prayed for someone, his hands would envelope that person's head like a skullcap. When he laid his hands on my head, I remember thinking, *There is no way God isn't going to answer his prayer*. He had a familiarity with God that was disarming. He had a faith in God that was reassuring.

He could have called a staff member to make the visit; he didn't. He could have waited until morning; he didn't. He sacrificed a full night's sleep to pray for a thirteen-year-old kid who was fighting for his life.

Little did he know that this thirteen-year-old kid would one day marry his daughter. Little did he know that this thirteen-year-old kid would one day give him his first grandchild, a colicky baby boy named Parker. There is no way he could have ever known, but that is the glorious mystery of prayer.

You never completely know who you are praying for and who is praying for you. You never know *how* or *when* God will answer your prayers. But you can be sure of this: *Your prayers will shape the destiny of your family for generations to come.* And if you are willing to interrupt your sleep cycle, if you are willing to get on your knees and intercede for your family, God will answer your prayers long after you are long gone.

Don't lose heart.

Don't lose hope.

Don't lose faith.

Keep circling!

Notes

Page 27: *mercy of the LORD*: Psalm 103:17 NKJV.

Page 27: *secured every spiritual blessing as our inheritance*: Ephesians 1:3.

Page 29: *The Israelites circled the city of Jericho*: Joshua 5:13 – 6:21.

Page 32: *"Lord, save me from the pit"*: Psalm 69:15 LB.

Page 32: *"Is anyone among you sick?"* James 5:14 ESV.

Page 34: *serve children with special needs*: To connect with the Johnsons or to track what God is doing with Connor, visit their website at www.connor moments.com (accessed March 15, 2012).

Page 40: *40 percent of our lives are based on personal prophecies*: Laurie Beth Jones, *The Power of Positive Prophecy: Finding the Hidden Potential in Everyday Life* (New York: Hyperion, 1999), ix.

Page 40: *You need to speak words of comfort*: 1 Corinthians 14:3.

Page 45: *Our true identity will only be revealed*: Revelation 2:17.

Page 52: *Delight yourself in the LORD*: Psalm 37:4 NASB.

Page 57: *The study did show one area*: Paco Underhill, *Why We Buy: The Science of Shopping*, rev. ed. (New York: Simon and Schuster, 2008), 111.

Page 58: *God will give them the ears of Samuel*: 1 Samuel 3:1–10.

Page 67: *If you ever drop your keys*: Jack Handey, *Deeper Thoughts: All New, All Crispy* (New York: Hyperion, 1993), 3.

Page 69: *When Jesse looked at David*: 1 Samuel 16:1–13.

Page 72: *The voice we should listen to most*: Frederick Buechner, *Secrets in the Dark: A Life in Sermons* (San Francisco: HarperOne, 2006), 40.

Page 72: *child to be "strong and courageous"*: Joshua 1:9; 1 Kings 15:5 (and many other verses).

Page 78: *Study done by a group of Utah researchers*: Julianne Holt-Lunstad, Wendy A. Birmingham, and Kathleen C. Light, "Influence of a 'Warm Touch' Support Enhancement Intervention Among Married Couples on Ambulatory Blood Pressure, Oxytocin, Alpha-Amylase, and Cortisol," *Psychosomatic Medicine* 70 (2008): 976-85.

Page 80: *"Unless you change and become like little children"*: Matthew 18:3.

Page 85: *Remember the story of Aaron and Hur*: Exodus 17:8–16.

Page 91: *Blessed is the one who is not offended*: Luke 7:23 ESV.

Bible Versions Cited

The Circle Maker

Praying Circles
Around Your
Biggest Dreams and
Greatest Fears

Mark Batterson

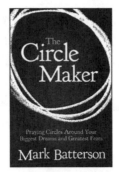

According to Pastor Mark
Batterson, "Drawing prayer
circles around our dreams isn't just a mechanism
whereby we accomplish great things for God. It's
a mechanism whereby God accomplishes great
things in us."

Do you ever sense that there is far more to
prayer and to God's vision for your life than
what you're experiencing? It's time you learned
from the legend of Honi the circle maker — a man
bold enough to draw a circle in the sand and not
budge from inside it until God answered his
prayers for his people.

What impossibly big dream is God calling you
to draw a prayer circle around? Sharing inspir-
ing stories from his own experiences as a circle
maker, Mark Batterson will help you uncover
your heart's deepest desires and God-given
dreams and unleash them through the kind of
audacious prayer that God delights to answer.

*Available in stores
and online January 2012!*

The Circle Maker Participant's Guide with DVD

Trusting God with Your Biggest Dreams and Greatest Fears

Mark Batterson

This four-session video-based study helps participants gain a deeper understanding of prayer and, in turn, make a more consistent practice of prayer. It will give viewers new vocabulary and methodology to pray with a holy confidence and will help them dream big, pray hard, and think long. The video sessions combine teaching elements with creative elements to draw viewers into the circle. Pack includes one softcover participant's guide and one DVD.

Session Titles:
The Legend of the Circle Maker
The 1st Circle: Dream Big
The 2nd Circle: Pray Hard
The 3rd Circle: Think Long

Also available: Curriculum Kit

*Available in stores
and online January 2012!*

Find Mark online at www.markbatterson.com,
on Facebook at www.facebook.com/markbatterson,
and on Twitter @MarkBatterson.

Share Your Thoughts

With the Author: Your comments will be forwarded to the author when you send them to *zauthor@zondervan.com*.

With Zondervan: Submit your review of this book by writing to *zreview@zondervan.com*.

Free Online Resources at
www.zondervan.com

Zondervan AuthorTracker: Be notified whenever your favorite authors publish new books, go on tour, or post an update about what's happening in their lives at www.zondervan.com/authortracker.

Daily Bible Verses and Devotions: Enrich your life with daily Bible verses or devotions that help you start every morning focused on God. Visit www.zondervan.com/newsletters.

Free Email Publications: Sign up for newsletters on Christian living, academic resources, church ministry, fiction, children's resources, and more. Visit www.zondervan.com/newsletters.

Zondervan Bible Search: Find and compare Bible passages in a variety of translations at www.zondervanbiblesearch.com.

Other Benefits: Register to receive online benefits like coupons and special offers, or to participate in research.

ZONDERVAN.com/
AUTHORTRACKER
follow your favorite authors